Musical Families

Around the World
with the Percussion Family!

by Trisha Speed Shaskan

illustrated by Robert Meganck

PICTURE WINDOW BOOKS
a capstone imprint

Special thanks to our advisers for their expertise:

Rick Orpen, PhD, Professor of Music, Gustavus Adolphus College
Terry Flaherty, PhD, Professor of English, Minnesota State University, Mankato

Picture Window Books
151 Good Counsel Drive
P.O. Box 669
Mankato, MN 56002-0669
877-845-8392
www.capstonepub.com

Editor: Jill Kalz
Designer: Lori Bye
Art Director: Nathan Gassman
Production Specialist: Jane Klenk
The illustrations in this book were
created digitally.

Printed in the United States of America in North Mankato, Minnesota
032010
005740CGF10

All books published by Picture Window Books
are manufactured with paper containing at least
10 percent post-consumer waste.

Library of Congress Cataloging-in-Publication Data
Shaskan, Trisha Speed, 1973–
Around the world with the percussion family! / by Trisha Speed Shaskan
; illustrated by Robert Meganck.
p. cm. — (Musical families)
Includes index.
ISBN 978-1-4048-6044-5 (library binding)
1. Percussion instruments—Juvenile literature. I. Meganck, Robert.
II. Title.
ML1030.S53 2011
786.8'19—dc22   2010001094

The word *percussion* means "the hitting of one thing against another." Percussion instruments make sounds when they're struck by another object.

Even though we belong to the same family, we each make a different sound. We provide the rhythm for music.

Turn the page to learn more about each of us and see some of the places we've been. My family and I have traveled all around the world!

5

One and two and three and four! Snare drums are great at tapping and rolling out rhythm. I have eight wires stretched across the bottom of my drum. The wires, called snares, are tightened to make the best sound.

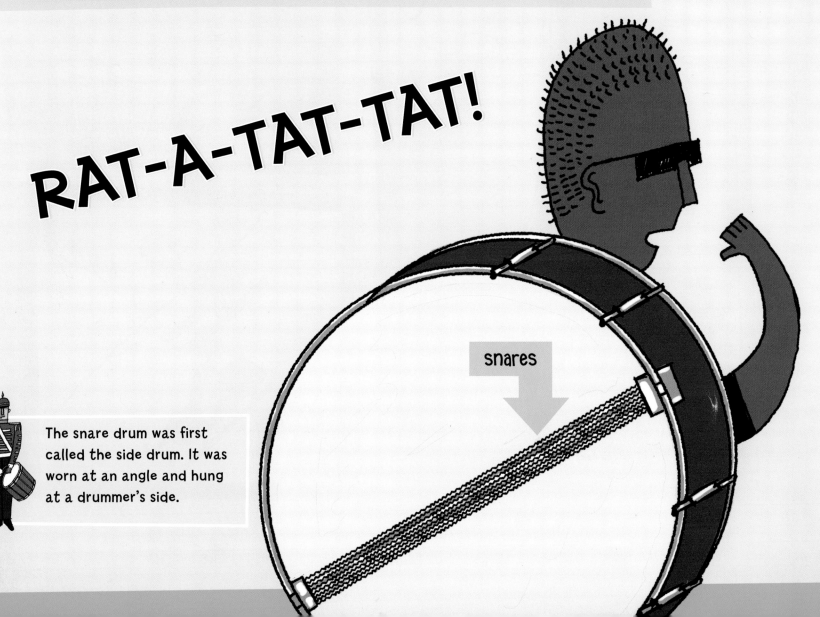

RAT-A-TAT-TAT!

snares

The snare drum was first called the side drum. It was worn at an angle and hung at a drummer's side.

This is my great-uncle Halim. My family visited him in Turkey last year. He marched in a band dressed like a snare drum from the 1700s. He even did tricks with his drumsticks.

Dad is the largest drum in the orchestra. Bass drums have two drumheads—one on each end. Musicians hit the drumheads with soft-headed sticks, or mallets.

drumhead

BOOM!
BOOM!

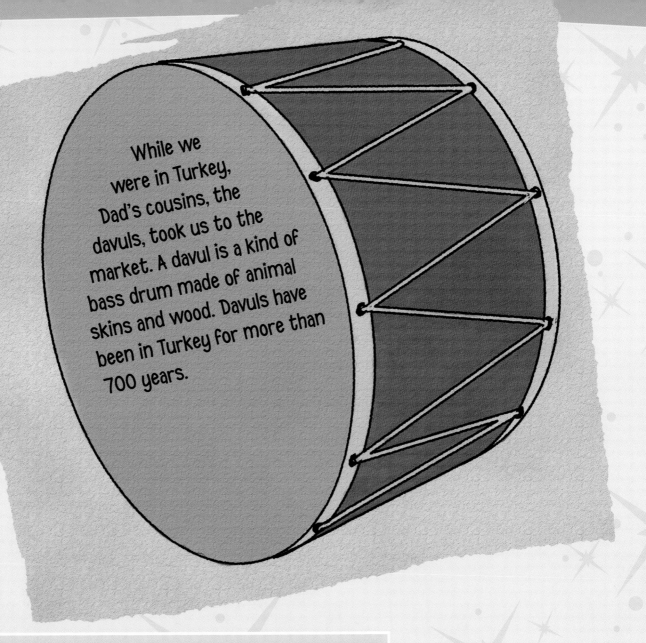

While we were in Turkey, Dad's cousins, the davuls, took us to the market. A davul is a kind of bass drum made of animal skins and wood. Davuls have been in Turkey for more than 700 years.

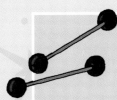
Sometimes a musician uses a double-headed stick to play the bass drum. He moves his wrist back and forth quickly so that each head hits the drum.

Mom's side of the family is all metal. Cymbals are made of copper and tin. When my mom wants to get the family's attention, she makes a loud

CRASH!

When Mom was younger, she played in a dance band, a marching band, and even an orchestra. Like all cymbals, Mom loves to travel. She's played in more countries than I can count!

My sister, Tina, is quite an instrument. Timpani create rhythm *and* melody. They strike the beats and sing the songs.

DUN-DUN-DUN-DUN!

Timpani are a pair of kettledrums. The head of each drum is stretched over a copper bowl, or kettle.

A musician presses a foot pedal to tune the drums. The pedal tightens or loosens the drumheads. Each drum has its own pitch.

Timpani drumsticks, called mallets, are wrapped in felt or leather.

Two years ago, my family visited France. We saw an amazing painting of one of our earliest relatives. Sir Henry Kettledrum was the first timpani in Europe. He was a military man.

We even have relatives in India! This is my great-aunt Kareena.
I think my sister looks a lot like her. Great-aunt Kareena doesn't
always ride camels and elephants—just on special days.

My brother Keys looks different from the rest of us. I call him Skeleton because his wooden bars remind me of bones. When struck, the bars move back and forth very quickly and make sound. Each bar plays a different note.

PLINK!
PLINK!
PLINK!
PLINK!

On a xylophone, the longest bars make the lowest sounds. The shortest bars make the highest sounds. The bars are tuned to make a scale.

Xylophones first came from Asia. And Japan was one of our most magical trips. Mom's cousin Aya introduced us to kabuki music. Kabuki is a kind of musical theater.

Baby Jangle is such a happy instrument. Tambourines are made of a hoop covered by a papery head. Metal discs, called jingles, are set into the hoop. When a musician shakes a tambourine, the jingles move and make sound.

JINGLE! JINGLE!

jingle

On our visit to Egypt, we saw dancers dressed like
ancient frame drums from 1550 BC. It was cool.
They looked just like Baby Jangle!

CRASH! CRASH!

BOOM!
BOOM!

JINGLE!
JINGLE!

In an orchestra, the percussion
section sits in the back.

21

I can't wait until our next vacation! Where will the Percussion family go next?

Glossary

melody—the series of notes that make up the main part of a song

musician—a person who plays music

orchestra—a group of musicians who play together on various instruments, especially violins and other string instruments

pitch—how high or low a sound is

rhythm—a pattern of beats

scale—a series of notes that go up and down in pitch

tune—to change to the right pitch

Fun Facts

Every country in the world has some kind of percussion instrument.

Finger cymbals make a small, bell-like sound. Middle-Eastern dancers often play them. A dancer wears one cymbal on her thumb and another cymbal on her middle finger.

The drum is thought to be the world's oldest instrument.

French composer Camille Saint-Saëns first used the xylophone in an orchestra in 1874. He used it to make the sound of rattling bones.

Bells, chimes, triangles, and gongs are members of the percussion family. So are rattles, wood blocks, bongo drums, and even whistles.

To Learn More

More Books to Read

Knight, M.J. *Percussion.* Musical Instruments of the World. North Mankato, Minn.: Smart Apple Media, 2006.

Koscielniak, Bruce. *The Story of the Incredible Orchestra.* Boston: Houghton Mifflin Co., 2000.

Witmer, Scott. *Drums, Keyboards, and Other Instruments.* Rock Band. Edina, Minn.: ABDO, 2009.

Internet Sites

FactHound offers a safe, fun way to find Internet sites related to this book.

All of the sites on FactHound have been researched by our staff.

Here's all you do:

Visit *www.facthound.com*

FactHound will fetch the best sites for you!

Index

24

Look for all the books in the Musical Families series:

Around the World with the
   Percussion Family!

The Brass Family on Parade!

The Keyboard Family Takes Center Stage!

Opening Night with the Woodwind Family!

The String Family in Harmony!

MERCURY

Susan Ring

MEDIA ENHANCED BOOKS
AV²
BY WEIGL™
ADDED VALUE • AUDIO VISUAL

www.av2books.com

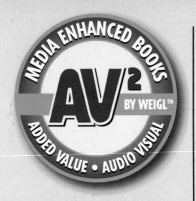

MEDIA ENHANCED BOOKS
AV²
BY WEIGL™
ADDED VALUE • AUDIO VISUAL

AV² provides enriched content that supplements and complements this book. Weigl's AV² books strive to create inspired learning and engage young minds in a total learning experience.

Your AV² Media Enhanced books come alive with...

Audio
Listen to sections of the book read aloud.

Key Words
Study vocabulary, and complete a matching word activity.

Video
Watch informative video clips.

Quizzes
Test your knowledge.

Embedded Weblinks
Gain additional information for research.

Slide Show
View images and captions, and prepare a presentation.

Try This!
Complete activities and hands-on experiments.

Go to www.av2books.com, and enter this book's unique code.

BOOK CODE

W 1 4 9 6 7 6

AV² by Weigl brings you media enhanced books that support active learning.

... and much, much more!

Published by AV² by Weigl
350 5th Avenue, 59th Floor
New York, NY   10118
Website: www.av2books.com   www.weigl.com

Library of Congress Cataloging-in-Publication Data

Ring, Susan.
 Mercury / Susan Ring.
   p. cm. -- (Our solar system)
 Includes index.
 Audience: 3-5.
 ISBN 978-1-62127-266-3 (hardcover : alk. paper) -- ISBN 978-1-62127-275-5 (pbk. : alk. paper)
 1. Mercury (Planet)--Juvenile literature. I. Title. II. Series: Our solar system (AV2 by Weigl)
 QB611.R562 2014
 523.41--dc23
                        2012040559

Printed in the United States of America in North Mankato, Minnesota
1 2 3 4 5 6 7 8 9 0   17 16 15 14 13

032013
WEP300113

Editor Kelley Kissner
Designer Mandy Christiansen

Every reasonable effort has been made to trace ownership and to obtain permission to reprint copyright material. The publishers would be pleased to have any errors or omissions brought to their attention so that they may be corrected in subsequent printings.

Photo Credits
Weigl acknowledges Getty Images as its primary photo supplier for this title. Other sources: Dreamstime: page 5 (Hubble Telescope), 19; European Space Agency: page 17 (*BepiColumbo*); iStockphoto: page 6; NASA: page 17 (*MESSENGER*); Royal Astronomical Society/Science Source: page 18.

Contents

3

Introducing Mercury

Mercury is the second-closest planet to Earth. Despite Mercury's closeness to Earth, the Sun's glare and extreme heat make Mercury difficult to study. Only recently have **astronomers** been able to gather much information about this planet. Read on to learn more about this fascinating planet in Earth's **solar system**.

Mercury is the smallest planet in the solar system.

Mercury Facts

- Mercury is nicknamed the "Dead Planet" because no living things exist there.

- Mercury is located 36 million miles (58 million kilometers) from the Sun.

- A large **asteroid** struck Mercury about 4 billion years ago. It made a very large **crater** known as the Caloris Basin. This crater covers an area about the size of Texas.

- Some areas of Mercury have steep cliffs known as scarps.

- Mercury has a large iron **core**.

- Scientists think there may be ice at the bottom of some craters on Mercury. They believe the Sun's rays never reach these spots.

- There are three types of planets in the solar system: rocky planets, **Gas Giants**, and **Ice Giants**. Mercury is a rock planet.

Naming the Planet

Mercury moves around the Sun very quickly. It travels at a speed of 107,000 miles (172,000 km) per hour during its **orbit**. This is faster than any other planet in the solar system orbits the Sun. That is why Mercury was named after the Roman god of trade and travel. In Roman **mythology**, Mercury is known as a quick messenger.

In Greek mythology, the god Hermes is known as a quick messenger. Both Hermes and Mercury are often shown with wings on their helmets and sandals.

Missing Moon

Unlike most planets, Mercury has no moon. Venus is the only other planet in the solar system that has no moon. Some scientists believe that Mercury was once Venus's moon. They think that Mercury broke away from its orbit. This would explain why neither planet has a moon.

The surface of Mercury looks similar to the surface of Earth's Moon. Both are covered with craters.

Earth's Moon   Mercury

First Sightings

People have seen Mercury glowing in the sky for thousands of years. The first written record of Mercury is from 265 BC by a Greek astronomer named Timocharis.

In the late 1800s, Italian astronomer Giovanni Schiaparelli mapped Mercury's position in the sky. Schiaparelli observed Mercury through his telescope for seven years before mapping its location.

A ridge on the surface of Mercury was named after Schiaparelli in 1976.

Hot and Cold

Mercury has very little **atmosphere**. Its thin atmosphere cannot block the Sun's rays during the day and cannot hold the Sun's heat at night. For this reason, temperatures on Mercury can be very hot or very cold.

During the day, Mercury can be as hot as 800° Fahrenheit (427° Celsius). This is hot enough to melt some types of metal. Mercury's temperature depends on its closeness to the Sun during its orbit.

At night, the heat of the Sun quickly escapes the atmosphere. Mercury's temperature falls to as low as –300°F (–184°C).

Even though Mercury is the closest planet to the Sun, Venus is the hottest planet in the solar system. This is because Venus is surrounded by a thick layer of clouds that traps the Sun's heat.

Spotting Mercury

Mercury looks like a star in the sky. Unlike a star, Mercury has no light of its own. It reflects the light of the Sun.

In some years, the Sun, Earth, and Mercury line up in a row. At this time, Mercury **transits** across the Sun. As it travels, Mercury looks like a little black dot against the Sun. A telescope is needed to view Mercury's transit. To prevent eye damage, special eye protection must be worn when looking directly at the Sun.

Mercury transits the Sun about 13 times every 100 years.

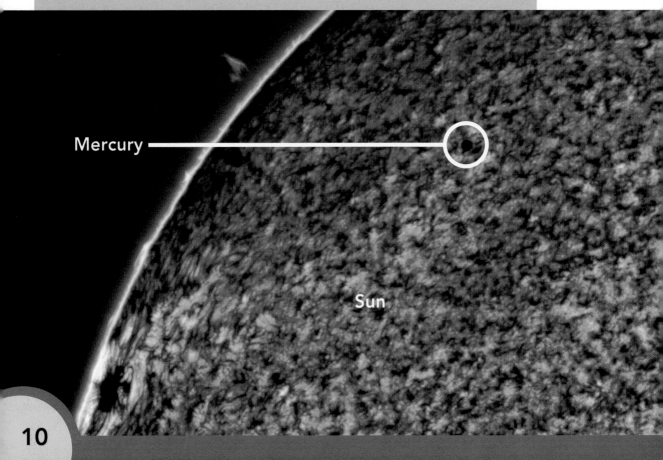

Mercury

Sun

See for Yourself

Mercury is visible if you look toward the **horizon**. It can be spotted just before sunrise and right after sunset. This is why Mercury has been called both the "morning star" and the "evening star."

In North America, Mercury is easiest to spot in the evenings during April and May. Even during these times, Mercury may be difficult to see in the sky. This is because dust in the atmosphere may limit its visibility.

Early Greek astronomers thought that Mercury was two objects in space because they could see it in the sky at two different times. They named these objects Apollo and Hermes.

Charting Our Solar System

Earth's solar system is made up of eight planets, five known dwarf planets, and many other space objects, such as asteroids and **comets**. Mercury is the closest planet to the Sun.

Sun

Mercury

Venus

Earth

Mars

Ceres

Jupiter

Order of Planets

Here is an easy way to remember the order of the planets from the Sun. Take the first letter of each planet, from Mercury to Neptune, and make it into a sentence. My Very Enthusiastic Mother Just Served Us Noodles.

Eris

Makemake

Haumea

Uranus

Pluto

Neptune

Saturn

Dwarf Planets

A dwarf planet is a round object that orbits the Sun. It is larger than an asteroid or comet but smaller than a planet.

Moons are not dwarf planets because they do not orbit the Sun directly. They orbit other planets.

Mercury and Earth

Mercury is much smaller than Earth. Eighteen objects the size of Mercury could fit inside Earth. Mercury also rotates more slowly on its **axis** than Earth. One rotation of Earth takes only 24 hours, or one day. It takes Mercury nearly 59 Earth days to complete one rotation.

By the time Mercury spins once on its axis, it has completed two-thirds of its orbit around the Sun.

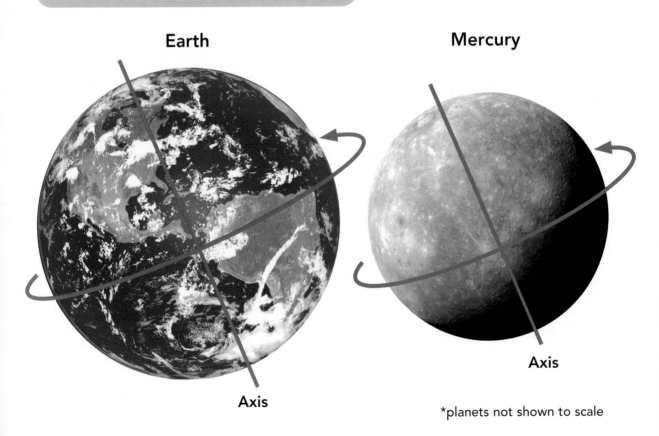

Earth

Mercury

Axis

Axis

*planets not shown to scale

Comparing the Planets

Planets (by distance from the Sun)	Distance from the Sun	Days to orbit the Sun	Diameter	Length of Day	Mean Temperature
Mercury	36 million miles (58 million km)	88 Earth days	3,032 miles (4,880 km)	1,408 hours	354°F (179°C)
Venus	67 million miles (108 million km)	225 Earth days	7,521 miles (12,104 km)	5,832 hours	847°F (453°C)
Earth	93 million miles (150 million km)	365 Earth days	7,926 miles (12,756 km)	24 hours	46°F (8°C)
Mars	142 million miles (228 million km)	687 Earth days	4,217 miles (6,787 km)	24.6 hours	−82°F (−63°C)
Jupiter	484 million miles (778 million km)	4,333 Earth days	88,732 miles (142,800 km)	10 hours	−244°F (−153°C)
Saturn	887 million miles (1,427 million km)	10,756 Earth days	74,975 miles (120,660 km)	11 hours	−301°F (−185°C)
Uranus	1,784 million miles (2,871 million km)	30,687 Earth days	31,763 miles (51,118 km)	17 hours	−353°F (−214°C)
Neptune	2,795 million miles (4,498 million km)	60,190 Earth days	30,775 miles (49,528 km)	16 hours	−373°F (−225°C)

Mercury Today

Only two **space probes** have flown by or orbited Mercury to study this planet. *Mariner 10* flew by Mercury three times after its launch in November 1973. This probe took photographs of about half of Mercury's surface.

MESSENGER was launched in August 2004. This probe flew by Mercury three times before it began to orbit the planet in March 2011. It is the first spacecraft to orbit Mercury. *MESSENGER* has photographed most of the surface of Mercury. It will continue to photograph and map Mercury's surface until at least 2013.

A third space probe to explore Mercury, *BepiColumbo*, is scheduled for launch in 2015. It will begin orbiting Mercury in 2022.

MESSENGER
Launched 2004
Vehicle Flyby and Orbiter

BepiColumbo
Launch 2015
Vehicle Orbiter

Mariner 10
Launched 1973
Vehicle Flyby

Planet Watchers

Eugenios Antoniadi mapped Mercury's surface

Eugenios Antoniadi (1870–1944) was a French astronomer. He studied Mercury through a powerful telescope. He was able to see Mercury more clearly than anyone ever had. Antoniadi created a detailed map of Mercury's surface in 1933. Some of the names of features on his map are still used today. In honor of his work, a long ridge on Mercury's surface was named after him in 1976.

A crater on Mars and a crater on Earth's moon have also been named after Antoniadi.

Maria Zuber helps guide Mercury mission

Maria Zuber is a teacher and scientist at the Massachusetts Institute of Technology. This is one of the world's top research universities. She teaches students about the solar system and the tools used to explore space.

Zuber and a team of scientists from **NASA** look at information collected by the *MESSENGER* space probe. She leads the group studying Mercury's surface and inner core.

Maria Zuber began building telescopes when she was only eight years old.

What Have You Learned?

Take this quiz to test your knowledge of Mercury.

1 How many moons does Mercury have?

2 What is the name of the first space probe to orbit Mercury?

3 There are many oceans on Mercury. True or False?

4 Is Mercury the closest or farthest planet from the Sun?

5 Who is Mercury named after?

6 The surface of Mercury is full of craters. True or False?

7 When is Mercury visible in the sky?

8 At what speed does Mercury travel in its orbit?

9 Which astronomer created a detailed map of Mercury's surface?

10 It is always cold on Mercury. True or False?

Young Scientists at Work

Mercury and the Sun

Early astronomers had trouble studying Mercury because of the Sun's glare. This experiment will show you how the Sun blocks our view of Mercury from Earth.

You will need:
- a lamp
- a pencil with printing on it

1. Hold the pencil up to the lamp's light. Then, turn the printed side of the pencil toward your eyes.

2. Now, try to read the writing on the pencil. Can you see the letters? You probably cannot. This is because the glare of the bright light prevents you from seeing the pencil's surface. This is similar to the effect the Sun has on our view of Mercury.

Key Words

asteroid: a small, solid object in space that circles the Sun

astronomers: people who study space and its objects

atmosphere: the layer of gases that surrounds a planet

axis: an imaginary line on which a planet spins

comets: small objects in space made from dust and ice

core: the center of a planet

crater: large pit or basin on the surface of a planet

Gas Giants: large planets made mostly of gas; Jupiter and Saturn are Gas Giants

horizon: an imaginary line where sky and ground seem to meet

Ice Giants: very cold giant planets; Neptune and Uranus are the two Ice Giants in the solar system

MESSENGER: Mercury Surface, Space ENvironment, GEochemistry, and Ranging

mythology: stories or legends, often about gods or heroes

NASA: National Aeronautics and Space Administration; part of U.S. government responsible for space research

orbit: the nearly circular path a space object makes around another object in space

solar system: the Sun, the planets, and other objects that move around the Sun

space probes: spacecrafts used to gather information about space

transits: travels across

Index

Log on to www.av2books.com

AV[2] by Weigl brings you media enhanced books that support active learning. Go to www.av2books.com, and enter the special code found on page 2 of this book. You will gain access to enriched and enhanced content that supplements and complements this book. Content includes video, audio, weblinks, quizzes, a slide show, and activities.

AV[2] Online Navigation

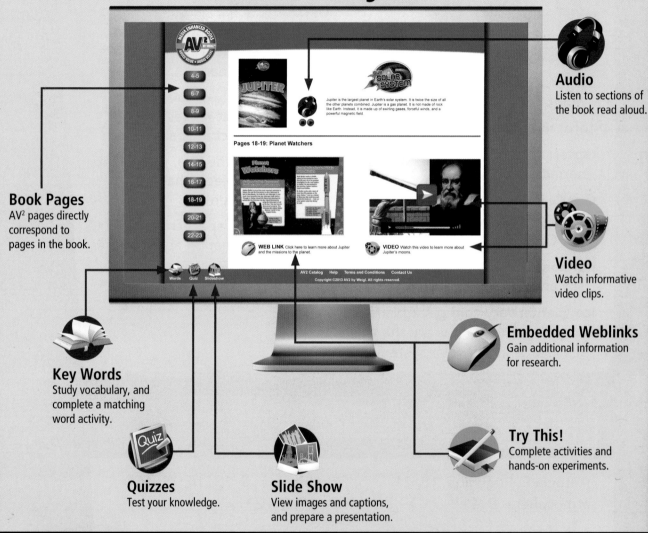

Audio
Listen to sections of the book read aloud.

Book Pages
AV[2] pages directly correspond to pages in the book.

Video
Watch informative video clips.

Key Words
Study vocabulary, and complete a matching word activity.

Embedded Weblinks
Gain additional information for research.

Quizzes
Test your knowledge.

Slide Show
View images and captions, and prepare a presentation.

Try This!
Complete activities and hands-on experiments.

AV[2] was built to bridge the gap between print and digital. We encourage you to tell us what you like and what you want to see in the future.

Sign up to be an AV[2] Ambassador at www.av2books.com/ambassador.